Library of Congress Cataloging-in-Publication Data

Hay, Louise L.
Loving thoughts for loving yourself / Louise L. Hay.
  p.   cm.
ISBN 1-56170-067-3 : $5.95
1. Love. 2. Self-acceptance. 3. Affirmations. I. Title.
BF575.L8H367 1993
158'.12--dc20   93-13179
                                                                CIP

Design & Typesetting by: Michele Lanci-Altomare

93 94 95 96 97 98 10 9 8 7 6 5 4 3 2 1
First Printing, September 1993

Published and Distributed in the United States by:
Hay House, Inc.
P.O. Box 6204
Carson, CA 90749-6204

♺

Printed in the United States of America
on Recycled Paper

Jose —
Read this daily
it works

LOVING THOUGHT

for

Loving Yourself

Louise L. Hay

---

love

Jane

Hay House
Carson, California

INTRODUCTION

The power of positive thinking is a well-known healing force even within the medical community. The positive, loving thoughts on the following pages are nothing more than positive affirmations.

You may feel that thinking a positive thought cannot possibly change your life, but how many times have you repeatedly affirmed a negative thought about yourself until finally it became true for you? Why not change those negative thoughts to positive ones?

I like to compare positive affirmations to planting a seed. You don't just plant the seed and get a beautiful flower the next day. It takes time. First you must water and nurture the seed and make sure it is safe from harm. It is the same with positive affirmations. You may not see changes immediately, but with enough nurturing and encouragement you can change your old negative way of thinking and look at things in a new and positive light.

Use these affirmations daily and over time you will begin to see your life turn in new direction and you will reap a bountiful harvest of positive, loving endeavors for yourself.

All is well,

Louise L. Hay

Today...

the love
in my world is a
mirror of the love
within me.

loving
relationships
begin with me.

Today...

I love
and cherish
myself.

TODAY...

I open
my heart
to myself.

Today...

I love myself
a little bit more.

TODAY...

love works
miracles in my life.

Today...

love is the most
powerful healing
force I know.

TODAY...

forgiveness has
opened the doorway
to my own love.

Today...

I help to create
a world where
it is safe to
love each other.

TODAY...

the more
love I give,
the more
love I receive.

Today...

and every day
loving gets easier.

TODAY...

events may come
and go,
but the love
for myself is
constant and true.

Today...

I dedicate this day
to loving myself
more.

TODAY...

wherever I go and
whoever I meet,
I always find love
waiting for me.

Today...

somewhere
someone is looking
for exactly what
I have to offer.

TODAY...

I attract more loving relationships into my life as I relax and accept myself exactly as I am.

Today...

it is safe
to let
the love in.

TODAY...

love is
my divine right.

Today...

I have
lots of friends
who love me.

TODAY...

when I really
love myself,
everything in
my life works.

I give myself
the gift of
unconditional
love.

the more
love I give
the more
I have to give.

Today...

when I look
into a mirror it is
easy for me to say,
"I love you.
I really love you."

TODAY...

there is
an endless well
of love within me
and I share it
with others.

I am
worthy of love.

loving myself
and others
gets easier.

Today...

I bless my parents
with love and
release them to
happiness that is
meaningful to them.

TODAY...

I have
a harmonious,
loving relationship
with all my family.

Today...

by sharing love
we can all live
in peace.

all is well
in my
loving world.

BOOKS IN THIS SERIES

Loving Thoughts for a Perfect Day
Loving Thoughts for Health and Healing
Loving Thoughts for Increasing Prosperity
Loving Thoughts for Loving Yourself

For a free catalog, call
1-800-654-5126

HAY
HOUSE